A Princess Called Brown Girl

Rev. Lisa Pate

Illustrated by
Toby Tober

Copyright ©2025 Lisa R. Pate, Listening Ear Publications
LisaPateMinistries.com
ListeningEarMinistries.com

Written by Lisa R. Pate

Illustrations by Toby Tober

Formatted and edited by Katie Erickson, KatieEricksonEditing.com

All rights reserved. No part of this publication may be reproduced, stored in a retrieval system or transmitted in any form or by any means, electronic, mechanical, including photocopying, recording or otherwise without prior written consent from the publisher.

Scripture quotations marked TPT are from The Passion Translation®. Copyright © 2017, 2018, 2020 by Passion & Fire Ministries, Inc. Used by permission. All rights reserved. ThePassionTranslation.com.

ISBN 978-1-7379706-3-7

This book belongs to:

_____

"Yes, he will soothe you with his love.
He will sing over you his song of praise."

Zephaniah 3:17 (TPT)

Dedication

This book is written for and dedicated to the presence of our "younger selves" – the precious younger self, who still reside in the hearts of young ladies, grown women, and senior women alike, especially for those of us who still long for the love, embrace and sweet glances of our father.

Let us be reminded that this book is not just a children's book. This is a loving memoir from our heavenly Father who chose us from the foundation of the earth. We were hand-picked, chosen, and preferred amongst many to be loved, cherished and embraced by God, our loving Heavenly Father.

He sings His Song of Love over you and me, here, now, and even forever.

This is the story of a beautiful princess, the daughter of a king, who was surrounded by others more beautiful than she. Some girls were of lighter or darker skin tones. There were those whose skin looked like the sun and those whose skin was like butter and just as smooth. There were those whose skin looked like freshly poured cream and those whose skin was like the color of tawny tan. Yes, there were those whose skin was as dark as coal and yet even more beautiful. There were those who were more beautiful than she, but she was Brown Girl – one who, through much turmoil, difficulty, and challenge, won the hearts of those who knew her story – the story of the Princess Called Brown Girl.

During a time of many dreams and wishes, there was a king whose name was King MeShullam. King MeShullam was not only kind, friendly, and quite approachable, but he was also filled with great joy. He sat joyously on his royal throne in his illustrious palace in a place far, far away.

The great and joyous king lived and celebrated life in his palace in Superia, the capital city of Beauty, in the Country of Utopia. Because of his kindness and generosity, he often celebrated his subjects with feasts for all his princes and courtiers. Not only did he take great joy in celebrating those who served him, but his first and highest joy was his family. His wife, Queen OriaKu, who was confident, courageous, and compassionate in her actions, reactions, and responses. King MeShullam loved Queen OraiKu. They were very happy together.

King MeShullam and Queen OraiKu had one son, Prince ShaKiah. The kind king and queen desired to have more children. After many years, decided to adopt a girl who would be a sister to Prince ShaKiah. With great kindness and love from their hearts, they agreed to adopt a blind child and love this child with all their hearts.

They named this beautiful child Princess SheKinah. She was initially very timid, fearful, and hesitant to receive the love that was lavishly poured out upon her, but over time and with much patience, King MeShullam, Queen OriaKu, and Prince Shakiah began to notice something so very beautiful about Princess SheKinah. Although she was born blind, she would often draw close to those whom she felt love through her listening ears. She would stand before them as though she could see them and hold out her arms as though receiving their love.

Both Prince ShaKiah and Princess SheKinah grew to love and adore one another as brother and sister. Even though there were years between them, you would have thought that they were twins. They were very sweet children and had many friends at the marketplace, where they would often visit with their Nanny-Mae.

During a recent visit to the marketplace, Princess SheKinah heard some girls of her age playing together and singing rhyming songs. Princess SheKinah loved to sing! She stood next to the young girls, eagerly wanting to be asked to join in with them to play and sing the songs that made their hearts so melodious. However, no one asked her to join in to sing the songs. Princess SheKinah began to look down. Her bright smile, which was always vibrant and radiant on her face, turned to a frown.

Her Nanny-Mae looked at her and asked, "Dear child, one who loves to smile, why do you frown?" She lifted her face up to Nanny-Mae and tried her hardest to smile. Instead, tears filled her eyes, and she blurted out with a force of passion that even she didn't know was within her, "Oh Nanny-Mae, I do want to sing the cheerful songs and play together with the other children in the marketplace. Tell me, what must I do?"

Nanny-Mae looked lovingly at Princess SheKinah, pulled her close to her with her loving arms, bent down, and whispered to her, "Beloved Princess Shekinah, you who are dearly loved by your father, who is the king, surely you know how to show love – even among those who may not know how to receive love."

A bright smile came to Princess SheKinah's face, a smile so bright it beamed with joy. Her eyes quickly began to sparkle with light and excitement because surely, she knew the treasure, the secret of her father's love. It was her greatest joy to show such love to everyone who may have never experienced this great love. Standing there in the marketplace, surrounded by the girls who previously did not allow her to join in with them singing songs, Princess SheKinah stood tall, held her head back, and with her arms wide open, she began to sing!

> "All who want to be loved, *COME*. All who desire to be touched and admired, *COME*. For everyone who wants to be happy, showing love is what makes one truly happy; showing love is what makes everyone happy, just *COME*."

Upon hearing Princess SheKinah sing the song from the top of her lungs, the little girls slowly stopped singing their songs. They all began to stand still and listen closely while Princess SheKinah stood even taller, it seemed, as she sang the song from her heart. For this was not a song that anyone had sung before. This song came from her father. It was a song he taught Prince ShaKiah and Princess SheKinah as they were readying for bed and experiencing his love and kindness. The king would sing this song to them both, especially on nights when he was leaving in the morning for a long trip.

> "All who want to be loved, *COME*. All who desire to be touched and admired, *COME*. For everyone who wants to be happy, showing love is what makes one truly happy; showing love is what makes everyone happy, just *COME*."

King MeShullam would take his very loving, long, and gentle arms and wrap them around both Prince ShaKiah and Princess SheKinah and whisper this song in their ears. Because they truly desired to be loved and admired, no matter how far he was away from them, they should simply COME to him – their loving father, who would give them all the love they needed.

The little girls in the marketplace listened to every word of the song as Princess SheKinah was singing, standing right in front of them with her arms stretched out as wide as the sky, singing melodiously. She sang it again and a third time, each time with even more passion than before.

> "All who want to be loved, *COME*. All who desire to be touched and admired, *COME*. For everyone who wants to be happy, showing love is what makes one truly happy; showing love is what makes everyone happy, just *COME*."

It was as though each word began resting on each little girl's ears. The melody and the words of Princess SheKinah's song began to capture their hearts as each word penetrated their ears and touched their very soul. Each girl was staring at Princess SheKinah.

Suddenly, each girl began swaying as Princess SheKinah was swaying to the melody of her own heart. Suddenly, each girl began slowly, from deep within their own selves, to sing the song, just as Princess SheKinah was singing it – not from memory but from their heart. Suddenly, each girl, while swaying and singing the song, began lifting their arms upward and then outward to embrace an unseen person – all while singing from the top of their lungs:

> "All who want to be loved, *COME*. All who desire to be touched and admired, *COME*. For everyone who wants to be happy, showing love is what makes one truly happy; showing love is what makes everyone happy, just *COME*."

Even the little boys who were nearby began swaying and singing the melodious song that Princess SheKinah had gladly taught her new friends. As each person began quieting themselves after finishing the song, they all began asking Princess SheKinah questions. What is your name? Where do you live? What are you doing here in the marketplace? When can you come again? Can you teach us another song?

Amid all the questions, Princess SheKinah gladly answered each and every one. She was excited about her new friends. While still fielding questions from them, she turned to Nanny-Mae and asked, "May we return again so that I can play with my new friends?"

Nanny-Mae happily suggested, "Princess SheKinah, not only will we return, but perhaps you would like to invite your new friends to your home for cake and punch one day soon?" Princess SheKinah took great delight in this suggestion and gladly told everyone, "Please, everyone, join me in the next few days in my backyard for a time of fun, cake, and punch!" Everyone was so very excited to do so.

When the day finally arrived for Princess SheKinah and her friends to enjoy an afternoon of cake and punch, the sun shined its brightest, the skies were their bluest and the robin birds which had a nest in her backyard, sang their sweetest.

It was such a joyous occasion that the only thing that could top this event was that Princess SheKinah had no idea that her father, the king, had changed his plans so that he could surprise her and attend the event instead of being told of the joyous time they all had.

To Princess SheKinah's surprise, all of her new friends began to arrive: her Asian friend Meing, whose skin was beautifully tawny tan, her Alaskan friend Aria, whose skin was beautifully creamy and her hair was black as night, her British friend Willow, whose eyes were green and delightfully covered by curly, red locks of hair, and her tallest friend Alubia from South Sudan whose skin was as dark as coal and her hair was curly just like Princess SheKinah's. She was surrounded by her friends! They were friends she had met just days before, but they had become friends of her heart.

As her friends were enjoying the lovely green, manicured lawn and the many colorful plants and flowers, they were surprised to see the array of animal shapes that were carved from wood, stone, and bushes. It was such a wonderful sight to behold. For they had never seen such vibrant colors, which were as many as a rainbow of candy.

Instead of serving cake and punch as suggested by Nanny-Mae, the king suggested a lavish meal for Princess SheKinah's friends. In fact, he said to Queen OriaKu, "Let's not only do a lavish meal. Let's surprise her, her friends, and Prince ShaKiah with an afternoon of our finest entertainment!"

Therefore, the queen had the king's chefs prepare the finest of food – the bite-sized burgers with smiles created from vegetables on the top of the burger buns and long and lean fries made from potatoes grown from the queen's garden, picked and washed just moments before cooking. The punch served was lemonade with a zing! The zing was freshly shaved ice and multi-colored ice cubes to make it fun to sip in the sun. The punch was served in tall, giraffe-shaped glasses with drinking straws that were the giraffe's neck.

It was fun to watch Princess SheKinah enjoying her friends who were all having such a refreshing time. The king had added so much more to this celebration; this is how kind and generous the king truly is. His kind and generous heart extended above and beyond what both Nanny-Mae and Princess SheKinah could ever have imagined.

As everyone had settled down and everyone's tummy was plump with the goodness of lunch, King MeShullam stepped out onto the patio and gave a very big and joyful welcome speech! "Welcome, friends of Princess SheKinah! You are welcomed into our home. My beloved Queen OraiKu and I welcome you with an abundance of joy, for it is our pleasure to have you join us for an afternoon of singing, dancing, and delightful fun!

With the wave of the king's hands, the entire landscape of the backyard was immediately filled with trampoline jumpers, trapeze artists, fireball throwers, short clowns, tall clowns, fat clowns, skinny clowns, and the friendliest lions, tigers, and bears.

It was a backyard circus of an enormous proportion! Smiles and great delight were on everyone's faces. Everyone was having such a wonderful time! As the sun began to set and the day's end drew near, the lions, tigers, and bears were sad to have to leave as they had a full fun-filled day of touching and being touched by their new friends Meing, Aria, Willow, and Alubia. The friendly animals had enjoyed their touch just as much as they had normally received touches from Princess SheKinah and Prince ShaKiah.

The animals were gently placed back into their places of rest, the trapeze artists stopped flying, the trampoline jumpers stopped jumping, all the fireball throwers put out their fires, and every short clown, tall clown, fat clown, and skinny clown was skirted away to their own humble abode. King MeShullam, Queen OraiKu, and their son Prince ShaKiah joined hands with Princess SheKinah and began to sing the song that brought everyone to the event:

> "All who want to be loved, *COME*. All who desire to be touched and admired, *COME*. For everyone who wants to be happy, showing love is what makes one truly happy; showing love is what makes everyone happy, just *COME*."

As the royal family began to sing and lift their voices, such wonderful harmony began to fill the yard. The harmony and the melody began to fill the trees, and it was as though the leaves began to blow in the wind to the sound and sway to the melody of every word. As the words of the song continued to rise within the trees, they could hear the branches swaying in the wind, and it sounded like the gentle clapping of hands. The royal family continued to sing. They, too, began to sway to the harmony of the song. One by one, slowly but surely, each friend – first Meing, then Aria, then Willow, and finally Alubia – all joined hands with the royal family, singing at the top of their lungs while swaying to the melodious sound of the beautiful words:

> "All who want to be loved, *COME*. All who desire to be touched and admired, *COME*. For everyone who wants to be happy, showing love is what makes one truly happy; showing love is what makes everyone happy, just *COME*."

As they continued to sing, sway, and lift their hands to the melodious sound, a gentle breeze began to blow and fill the space of the entire backyard. Everyone was enraptured by the words of the song. The beautiful words rested upon each of their hearts. As they sang, it was as though the words had wings and were flying to fill the air.

They sang gently and lovingly, and finally, the song came to an end. Beautiful Alubia spoke up and asked in broken English, "Why does my heart feel so very light? I feel as though I could float away into the skies." Queen OraiKu gently turned to Alubia and said to her, "Beloved Alubia, your burdens have been lifted. Whatever sorrows were sitting quietly within your heart – they have been put to rest now. You are now experiencing the blessing of stillness of heart – enjoy this place, beloved." Alubia nodded her long neck and her head in agreement. It was a beautiful blessing of stillness that enlightened her and everyone.

Soon, everyone was hugging, and joyful sounds once again filled the air. Princess SheKinah was glad that her friends had experienced her family as they joined in singing the song together. It was such a beautiful time of joy and celebration. But now, it was time to depart, and although she did not want them to go, she knew within her heart of hearts that she would be with them all again. She knew that Nanny-Mae would surely take her to the marketplace, but she knew that her family had enjoyed them all and would certainly welcome them back to the royal palace again and again.

As her new friends began to depart and leave the place where they had all enjoyed such a wonderful time together, each of her friends stood in the presence of Princess SheKinah. They were saying goodbye and wishing everyone well. But then Meing lifted her voice and asked a question that surprised everyone. "Prince ShaKiah, why does your sister, Princess SheKinah, look so different than you?" Prince ShaKiah turned to his father the king and looked as if to ask for permission to tell a timeless story. King MeShullam gently nodded his head as did Queen OraiKu.

Prince ShaKiah began to tell the story. "You see, Meing, our family could have ended with me being an only child, but it was my father and mother's pride and joy to have more children. Because heaven is so very good to its children, heaven delivered Princess SheKinah to my mother, the queen. She is an adopted and wonderfully loved sister of mine. My father, the king, and my mother, the queen, all have beautiful brown skin, and my beautiful sister's skin is darker brown, but she is the most precious to us in the Kingdom. Princess SheKinah is precious, not because she may seem to others to be different due to her darker skin and her sight being blind, but because she preciously and lavishly loves me, my father, my mother, and all the people of our kingdom. She was given to us by heaven's drops of love, and for that, we are eternally grateful! Her skin may be darker brown, but she has royal blood running in her veins, and we love her with everlasting love.

Yet, with her blindness, she sees everything at a greater measure than we ever will. My sister sees through the heart of love. She is our adopted, beautiful sister and daughter to my father, the king, and my mother, the queen. We not only love her but even more, we cherish her. Our father named her Princess SheKinah because the glory of Jehovah, our God, Master, and Lord, rests upon her life. For that, we are in adoration of who she is and all that she will ever do and forever grow into."

Prince ShaKiah continued, "For you see, my dear Meing, the song that drew you and all of my sister's friends here today was written by my father, the king, for my sister, Princess SheKinah! The beautiful and melodious song was written so that she could experience dear and true love. Once my father heard the words in his heart, he began singing them to her and to me, and a miracle took place! She began looking deeply into my father's eyes, longing for a father to come and bring deliverance to her and love her as the daughter she desperately desired to be.

"Even though she is blind, through love, she was able to see straight to my father's heart. Princess SheKinah allowed the words to rest upon and settle deep within her own heart first, which is why she can sing the song with such great joy, lifting her arms and holding her head back. She has experienced the great love of my father. Through these words, love has come to her, to me, and yes to you, Meing. Listen to the words and hear my dear sister singing them:"

> "All who want to be loved, *COME*. All who desire to be touched and admired, *COME*. For everyone who wants to be happy, showing love is what makes one truly happy; showing love is what makes everyone happy, just *COME*."

From that moment on, Princess SheKinah became known and loved all the more as Princess Brown Girl. For she truly was the daughter of the king and queen and sister to the generous and kind prince. Her friends near and far not only cherished her as Princess SheKinah but also as Princess Brown Girl – for her skin was beautifully chestnut brown, her eyes were a golden hue, although blind, and her hair was beautifully coiled with tresses of brown curls. She was a short, little, girl known as Princess Brown Girl!

The End

About the Author

Rev. Lisa Pate is first and foremost mom to her four cherished young adult children: Cornel and daughter in-love April, Israel, and Caleb. She is a Godly-proud grandmother to three beautiful grandchildren, Mylessa Anne, Riley Owen, and Issey Renee. Rev. Lisa, as she is affectionately known, is a licensed and ordained minister in the Church of God, Cleveland, TN, a published author, speaker, and Bible teacher.

About the Illustrator

Toby Tober has been drawing since he was young and loves creating illustrations that bring stories to life. He lives in Florida with his wife of 25 years, Rebecca. They have three children and a precious grandson. When he isn't drawing or painting custom wall murals, Toby enjoys playing guitar on his church's worship team.

www.ingramcontent.com/pod-product-compliance
Lightning Source LLC
Chambersburg PA
CBHW061358090426
42743CB00002B/58